# THE BUILDING BLOCKS OF SELF-ESTEEM

By Lawrence E. Shapiro, Ph.D.

**Designed and Illustrated by Christopher Laughlin**

D0731122

**Childswork/Childsplay**
Secaucus, New Jersey

**THE BUILDING BLOCKS OF SELF-ESTEEM**
Written by Lawrence E. Shapiro, Ph.D.
Designed and Illustrated by Christopher Laughlin
Edited by Hennie M. Shore

©1993 Childswork/Childsplay, LLC, a subsidiary of Genesis Direct, Inc.
100 Plaza Drive, Secaucus, NJ 07094.
All rights reserved.
Printed in the United States of America

ISBN 1-882732-08-1

SECOND PRINTING

## Other products by Childswork/Childsplay

**Play-and-Read Series Books**
ALL ABOUT DIVORCE
ALL FEELINGS ARE OK—IT'S WHAT YOU DO WITH THEM THAT COUNTS
FACE YOUR FEELINGS
TAKE A DEEP BREATH: The Kids' Play-Away Stress Book

**Self-Esteem Series Books**
SOMETIMES I DRIVE MY MOM CRAZY, BUT I KNOW SHE'S CRAZY ABOUT ME:
      A Self-Esteem Book for ADHD Children
SOMETIMES I LIKE TO FIGHT, BUT NOT MUCH ANYMORE
SOMETIMES I FEEL LIKE I DON'T HAVE ANY FRIENDS, BUT NOT MUCH
      ANYMORE

**Psychological Games**
MY TWO HOMES
STOP, RELAX & THINK
THE ANGRY MONSTER MACHINE
THE CLASSROOM BEHAVIOR GAME
THE DINOSAUR'S JOURNEY TO HIGH SELF-ESTEEM
THE GOOD BEHAVIOR GAME
THE GREAT FEELINGS CHASE
YOU & ME: A GAME OF SOCIAL SKILLS

For a free catalog of books, games and toys to help children, call 1-800-962-1141.

# Introduction

Few people would deny the important role of self-esteem in the growing child. However, equally few people would be able to describe exactly what self-esteem is and why it is important.

Many people, both in psychology and education, have confused *self-esteem* with *self-love*. It goes without saying that children should learn to "love," "care for," and "nurture" themselves as they internalize the roles once filled by their own parents. But taking care of oneself, even in the deepest meaning of this phrase, does not alone lead to high self-esteem. Rather, an over-concern with oneself and one's needs leads to narcissism and ego-centrism, which has nothing at all to do with self-esteem as a psychological concept.

Some leaders of the self-help movement have also contributed to this misunderstanding, suggesting that self-acceptance alone will lead to a high level of self-esteem. But while self-acceptance is important, it is just the beginning. At The Center for Applied Psychology, Inc., it is our belief that self-esteem must be viewed in a social context, and should be defined in terms of total personality development. From an educational or intervention perspective, we also believe that self-esteem can be defined in terms of specific traits and skills which can be learned at any age.

This activity book introduces self-esteem as a multi-dimensional concept, which is derived from at least six major dimensions: Affect, Behavior, Cognition, Development, Education, and Social System.

**Affect** refers to not only feeling good about oneself, but also to understanding and controlling one's entire range of feelings. Children need to learn the feelings associated with high self-esteem, as well as the ones that are associated with a poor self-image. Understanding the feelings of others will lead to being able to empathize with others, which in turn leads to closer relationships and feelings of intimacy.

An important factor in the self-esteem of children is how they are seen and treated by the important people in their lives, and this, in turn, is largely influenced by their behavior. Children who are polite, well-mannered, thoughtful, and responsible are almost always well-liked, and this strongly influences their sense of self. To put it simply, **behaving** in pro-social ways gets important positive feedback from others.

A significant portion of the research done on how children can "learn" to have a good image of themselves has concentrated on their **cognition** or thought patterns. Children with a high self-esteem seem to have learned specific cognitive traits of having self-reinforcing and self-motivating thoughts, as well as problem-solving and decision-making skills.

The **developmental** success of a child is often overlooked as an important contributor to self-esteem. Children who do not achieve certain developmental milestones may perceive themselves (and may be perceived by others) as inadequate. Consider the child who wets his bed or sucks his thumb beyond the age of four or five. Or the child who does not achieve certain social milestones, such as having a best friend, or being part of a structured peer group. In each instance, the child has not met both internal and external expectations of his age.

**Education**, which leads to a good self-image, particularly in terms of learning values, is an area which is often talked about, but less often addressed. Learning values must be an important part of each day, both at home and at school. Values should be defined in the broadest sense, to include both social values and responsibility, as well as the appreciation of aesthetics and beauty.

A child's **social system** must be defined as broadly as possible to include the influences of the home, school, community, and, of course, the child's peers. At each age the child will experience social influences and expectations from a different group of significant people, and the effect on the child's self-esteem is cumulative. The influence of our parents, our teachers, our early friends, as well as community figures will shape our sense of self-worth for a lifetime.

In *The Building Blocks of Self-Esteem*, we have tried to give you a sampling of activities, geared toward younger children, that illustrate the importance of each of these areas. We hope that this book will encourage you to find many more ways to encourage a child's self-esteem, and to provide the best foundation from which a child can build.

*– Lawrence E. Shapiro, Ph.D.*
*Childswork/Childsplay*

---

**What You Will Need:** The activities in this book can be easily copied for distribution to more than one child at one time. However, children will need some readily-available materials to complete them, including:

- Pencils
- Crayons
- Markers
- Paste

- Scissors
- Photographs
- Magazines
- 10 Pennies (for activity A-8)

To a large extent, having a positive self-image involves positive feelings about oneself. It would be nice if we could always feel "good," but in fact we have many feelings, some positive and some negative.

While we can't always feel "good," we can learn to understand and accept all our feelings, to communicate feelings appropriately, to understand the feelings of others, and to control our feelings appropriately so that they serve us in social situations and in achieving our goals.

Sometimes feelings can be expressed in colors. The color red usually means "anger," while blue is a soothing, calm color.

Color in the pictures on these pages to show how you feel about the different things that are pictured. Write in (or have someone else write in) your feelings about each picture.

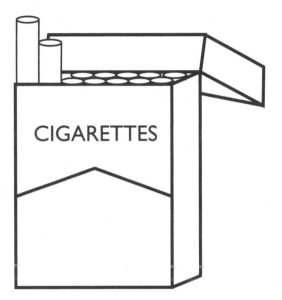

A-1

Sometimes we think that animals have feelings like we do. Grown-ups sometimes say:

*You're as shy as an ostrich.*

*You're as quiet as a mouse.*

*You're as brave as a lion.*

*You're a fraidy cat.*

*You're as gentle as a lamb.*

Can you draw a picture (or find one in a magazine) of the animal that you think is most like you?

A-2

Most of the time you can tell how people are feeling just by the way they look. The expression on a person's face and the way he moves and holds his body can tell you many things before he even says a word.

On the next four pages, paste photographs or pictures from magazines of people who are feeling these four basic emotions: **Sad**, **Mad**, **Happy** and **Scared**.

A-3

# SAD

# MAD

# HAPPY

# SCARED

**Area: Affect**
**Activity: The Best Picture Ever**
**Objective: To identify things that are associated with positive feelings.**

Fill this picture so that everything in it makes you feel good (older kids can draw in the picture; younger kids can paste in magazine cutouts).

- Draw in your favorite clothes.
- Put your favorite toys and books on the shelves.
- Put in your friends and family.
- Put in anything you like.

A-4

**Area: Affect**
**Activity: The Right Feeling in the Right Place**
**Objective: To understand that different feelings can be more (or less) appropriate in different situations.**

Sometimes different situations require you to have different feelings, even though those feelings may not seem natural. For example, if you have to sing or perform in front of an audience, you have to be brave, not afraid. Sometimes you have to force yourself to have the right feelings.

Here are some children with different feelings. Cut them out and paste them them in the right situations on the following pages. Color in the pictures if you like. Write (or have someone else write) the feeling that is necessary to make each situation come out all right.

A-5

How would you feel in this situation?

_____

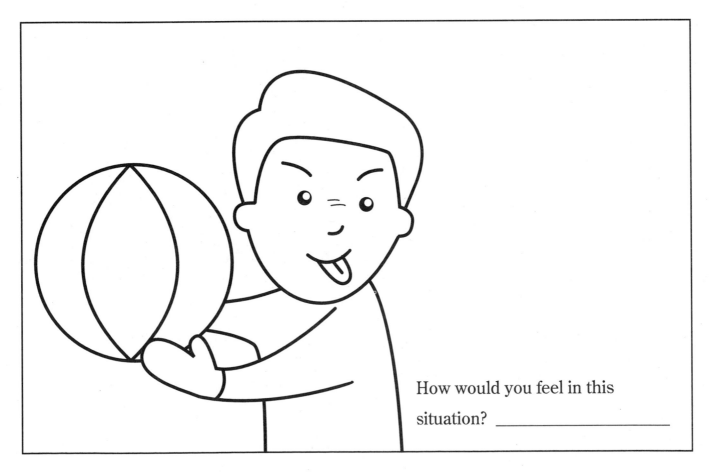

How would you feel in this

situation? _____

How would you feel in this situation?

_____

How would you
feel in this situation?

_____

How would you feel in this situation?

_____

How would you feel in this situation?

_____

Susan has had a terrible day and she is really unhappy. Circle at least five things that might have made her feel bad.

A-6

What can Susan do to cheer herself up?

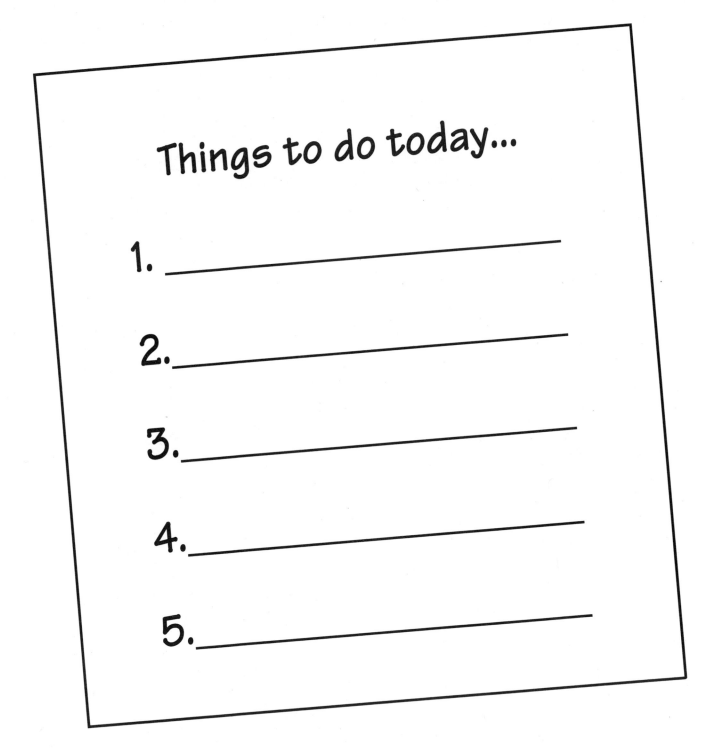

Things to do today...

1. _____

2. _____

3. _____

4. _____

5. _____

**Area:  Affect**
**Activity:  The Book of Good and Bad Feelings**
**Objective:  To help identify and understand the role of positive and
negative feelings and that different feelings can exist simultaneously.**

Get a notebook with at least 50 pages in it.  You are going to make it into
a "double book."

Fill in the pictures on the next page.  Paste one picture on the front cover of the
notebook and place the other picture upside down on the back cover.  Every day, for
at least two weeks, fill a page in your Good Feelings Book and then flip it over and fill
a page in your Bad Feelings Book.  You can write, draw, paste in pictures from
magazines, or paste in photographs.  That's up to you, but don't let a day go by
without thinking about your feelings!

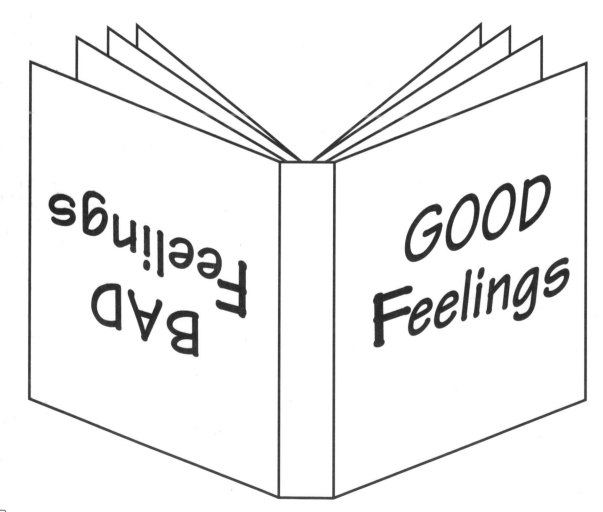

(Paste this picture on the front cover)

Things That Make Me Feel Good

(Paste this picture on the back cover, upside down,
so that you have a "double" book)

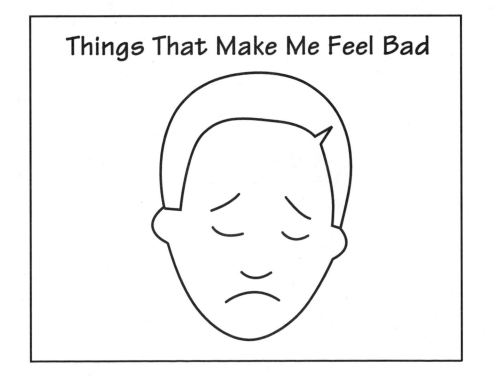

Things That Make Me Feel Bad

**Area: Affect**
**Activity: Learning About Anger**
**Objective: To help children learn appropriate ways to express anger and aggression.**
**You will need 10 pennies for this activity.**

Copy these two pages and/or cut them out of this book, then tape them together to form a target.

Take turns "pitching the pennies." The object is to get the pennies in circles that have a higher point value. To get the points, you must correctly answer the questions in the circles or perform the required act.

Once each player has 50 points, he or she wins and should get a reward.

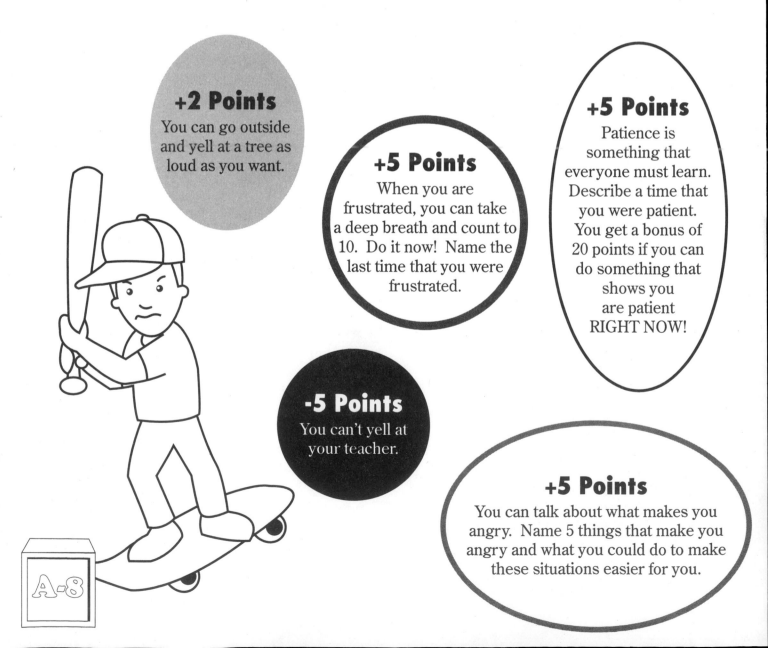

### +2 Points
You can go outside and yell at a tree as loud as you want.

### +5 Points
When you are frustrated, you can take a deep breath and count to 10. Do it now! Name the last time that you were frustrated.

### +5 Points
Patience is something that everyone must learn. Describe a time that you were patient. You get a bonus of 20 points if you can do something that shows you are patient RIGHT NOW!

### -5 Points
You can't yell at your teacher.

### +5 Points
You can talk about what makes you angry. Name 5 things that make you angry and what you could do to make these situations easier for you.

A-8

## +2 Points

You can hit your pillow as hard as you like.

## +2 Points

You can wrestle with children your size, if you are careful not to hurt anyone, and you follow safety rules.

## -2 Points

You can't hit other children.

## +5 Points

Take a mirror and smile at yourself. Now think about the thing that makes you the most angry in the whole world. Keep smiling. Think harder. Keep smiling. Think harder. KEEP SMILING!

## -2 Points

You can't play too rough with other children.

## +5 Points

You can respect other people's feelings. See if you can remember a time when you did not control your anger. How did the other person feel?

FUN TIME

## Discussion Questions

1.  Name as many feelings as you can in just one minute.

2.  Who do you know who is *happy* most of the time?

3.  Name someone on TV who is *afraid* most of the time.

4.  What is the one thing that really makes you sad?

5.  Play a song that makes you really happy. Now do a dance that shows how you feel!

6.  What is the worst feeling you ever had? Why did you feel that way?

7.  How do you know when someone is mad at you if she doesn't tell you? Make a "mad" face in the mirror. Take a pose (like a statue) to show that you are mad. Do you know anyone who "shows" his feelings but doesn't talk about them?

8.  There once was a little boy named Tommy Temper. He was mad as soon as he got up, at breakfast, at school, at home, and when he went to bed. He was mad all the time. Then one day he woke up, and he wasn't mad anymore. What in the world do you think happened to Tommy to change his feelings?

9.  When you are sad, or feel bad, name four things that make you feel better.

10. Sometimes people feel two or more different feelings at the same time, like when you are on a roller coaster and you are scared and excited at the same time. Or when it is your birthday and the party is over. You feel happy, but you may be sad that your birthday is almost over. Can you think of a time when you felt two different feelings at the same time?

Self-esteem is thought to come from our inner thoughts and feelings, but our inner-self is shaped and influenced by outside forces. When we feel that people like us, we, in turn, like ourselves.

It is clear that children as well as adults respond to kids who behave well; kids who are polite, well-mannered, thoughtful, and responsible. When you encourage good behavior in children, you support actions and habits which will win them praise, affection, and approval, and which will, in turn, translate into a solid foundation for building self-worth.

**Area:** Behavior
**Activity:** Looking Good!
**Objective:** To differentiate between good and bad behaviors.

People who feel good about themselves have good behaviors. Everyone likes them because they are polite and considerate of others.

Color the children in the picture who are behaving the way the teacher wants them to behave.

TOYS

B-1

The Sloppy family is having one of its typical family meals. They wanted to invite some guests, but nobody likes to come over to visit them. It's no wonder why!

Can you find 12 things that are wrong with this picture? (The answers are written upside down at the bottom of this page).

B-2

Answers: 1) *dirty dishes* 2) *Dad reading newspaper at table* 3) *food fell off plates* 4) *spilled milk* 5) *spilled drink off table* 6) *baby on floor with food* 7) *messy toys* 8) *TV on during meal* 9) *papers on floor* 10) *Girl brushing hair at table* 11) *Boy with elbows on table* 12) *Boy playing with food*

**Area: Behavior**
**Activity: Family Manners Matter**
**Objective: To understand the importance of manners in the family.**

Name the three most important manners in your family.

1. ______________________________

2. ______________________________

3. ______________________________

Cut out this award and give it to the person you know who has the best manners.

## • BEST MANNERS AWARD •

**(Name)** ______________________

**has the**

# BEST MANNERS

**of anyone I know.**

**(Signed)** ______________________

**Area: Behavior**
**Activity: Teaching Earthling Rules**
**Objective: To understand the importance of responsible behavior.**

Erjon just arrived on Earth from another planet. The first thing he must do is learn right from wrong. Can you help him? Draw a line from the rules that are "right" to Erjon's notebook. Draw a line from the rules that are "wrong" to the trash can (he won't need those). How many rules were right and how many were wrong?

. . . . . . . . . . . . . . . . . . . . . . . . . . . . . . . . . . . . . . . . . . . . . . . . . . .

Treat everyone with respect.

If you have trash, just throw it on the ground.

If you see something you want in a store, just take it.

Never hit people or animals.

Don't interrupt when other people are speaking.

Don't chew with your mouth open.

If you don't like school, don't bother going.

Don't cross the street without looking.

Eat food that is good for you and
    get the right amount of sleep.

Eat ice cream until you feel sick.

Work hard in school.

Watch television as much as you want.
    It's good for you.

Erjon's Notebook

B-4

Sometimes kids don't understand adult rules that keep them from having fun. Why can't Jim eat all his Halloween candy? Why can't Keisha stay in the pool a little longer if she wants to? Adults often have to put limits on children for many reasons...most of them good ones. Can you match the mixed-up scenes below? Draw a line from the boxes on the left to the correct boxes on the right to see what rules these children are breaking.

**Area: Behavior**
**Activity: It's Your Job to be Responsible**
**Objective: To understand the importance of responsible behavior.**

Most kids know that they have to be responsible for themselves. They have to brush their teeth, eat good food, exercise, and do things that will help them grow up to be strong and smart.

Kids also have to be responsible to their families. They have to do chores, obey rules, and consider the feelings of other family members.

And kids have a greater responsibility, as well, to their community and even to the planet. When we help others, we help ourselves as well.

Here are some things that can help you do your job to be responsible to yourself, your family, and the people around you. Write (or have someone else write) what you can do with each object.

SOAP

WINDOW CLEANER

B-6

Name _____

**Area: Behavior**
**Activity: You're the Judge**
**Objective: To understand different kinds and degrees of punishment.**

Kids don't like being punished, but did you know that adults also get in trouble if they do something wrong? They get a ticket if they speed in their car. They get fired from their jobs if they are always late. If they don't pay their taxes, the government can take money from their bank accounts and make them pay extra money too! Punishments are different depending on the law that was broken.

Most people think that punishments for kids should be different too, depending on what they did. Cut out the gavels on the next page and paste them next to each rule that was broken below. You decide how each child should be punished.

Tom pushed his little sister.

Mary didn't do her homework.

Bobby didn't take out the trash.

David stole candy from his friend's house.

Sally "faked" being sick to stay home from school.

Larry didn't clean up his room.

Rhonda talked back to her mother.

Caren threw a tantrum over a dress that she wanted.

Ron said his little brother broke the TV, but he did it.

B-7

Tyler stole baseball cards from the store.

Gerald cheated at a game.

Tanya came to dinner late every night for a week.

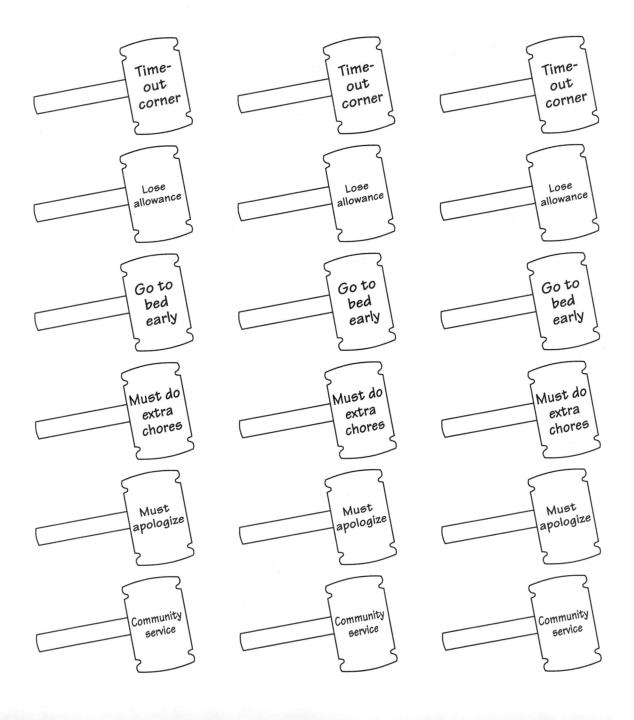

Tim wanted to make some extra money so that he could buy a model plane that he saw in a store. But he doesn't know what to do. Can you think of four ways that Tim could make money? They are right in front of his eyes.

B-8

Grown-ups make the rules. That's just the way it works. But kids often have good ideas about rules too! What are some fair rules that you would make if you had your own rule book? Write them in the spaces below. Do you think you should tell a grown-up about some of your rules?

## Kids' Rule Book

1. _____

2. _____

3. _____

4. _____

5. _____

6. _____

7. _____

8. _____

9. _____

10. _____

The way you look shows a lot about how you feel inside. Here is a fun game to play using another person like he or she was a large doll. Have him or her stand in front of the other players. Then pick one of the "Feelings Boys" and shape the person to look like one of them. The other players must guess the feeling.

**ANGRY**

**HAPPY**

**SAD**

**PROUD**

**AFRAID**

B-10

## Discussion Questions

1. What did you do this week to help someone else?

2. Why is it important to keep your room clean?

3. Name three ways that children should show respect for older people.

4. What is the most important rule that you would teach a younger child?

5. What do you think is the most important rule that grown-ups must follow?

6. John sometimes told lies. He lied to his mother about doing his homework. He lied to his teacher about being late for class. He lied to his best friend, Larry, when he crashed Larry's bike. What would you tell John about lying?

7. Name the chores that you do around your house. What do you think is the most important thing that you do for your family?

8. What is the most important rule that *grown-ups* should not break?

9. Ask some grown-ups about what happened to them when they broke rules. How were they punished?

10. What happens when a child breaks an important rule in your class?

People with high self-esteem have developed a way of thinking about themselves and the world which focuses on the positive instead of the negative. This style of thinking involves a combination of positive attitudes, self-motivation, independent thought, and self-encouragement. Much of the self-help movement has focused on helping people to have a positive and supportive "internal dialogue;" inner thoughts which encourage and "affirm" one's self-worth.

Developing a positive inner-dialogue is a skill that can be taught to children, just as other cognitive skills can be taught, including planning ahead, problem-solving, decision-making, and so on. Cognitive skills which result in successful goal-oriented behavior contribute most effectively to a child's sense of well-being.

Everybody dreams of being a super-hero with special super powers. If you could have just one super power, what would it be? What would you do with it?

Draw in the super power you want the kids below to have. For example:

X-Ray eyes
Super strength (lots of muscles)
Super hearing (big ears)
Super speed ( wings on their feet)
and so on.

What would you do with your own super power?

_____

_____

_____

What real power do you already have that you think is special?

_____

C-1

Sometimes when things are bad, you can remember times that were really good and that can cheer you up. When Charles had to go to the doctor to get a shot, he always thought about ice cream. He'd imagine that he was sitting in a huge bowl of vanilla ice cream, flowing over with sticky hot fudge. By the time he was finished taking his ice cream bath (and eating it too) the shot was all over.

What would you think of to cheer yourself up if something was making you unhappy? Write it in the "thought balloon" below.

When would you use this thought to cheer yourself up?

C-2

**Area:  Cognition**
**Activity:  You Can Get Straight A's in What You Do Best.**
**Objective:  To identify the things at which a person excels.**

Did you know that anyone can get a perfect report card?  It could happen if you got grades in what you're already good at!  Fill in the report card below, choosing the things that you do really well.  It could be anything, like reading or math, or playing ball or video games, or just playing!  What you're good at is an important part of who you are.

# REPORT CARD

Name _____

| Subject | Comments | Grade |
|---------|----------|-------|
|         |          | A+    |
|         |          | A+    |
|         |          | A+    |
|         |          | A+    |
|         |          | A+    |
|         |          | A+    |

C-3

This boy wants to get his ball, but he is afraid of the dog in the yard. The dog can't get loose–he is chained and behind a fence–but the boy is afraid anyway.

Can you think of three things that this boy can say to himself that will help him be brave enough to get his ball? Write them below.

1. _____

2. _____

3. _____

C-4

Donna has a lot of homework to do, but her friend Martha has invited her to come over and play with her new computer game. How can Donna decide what to do?

When people have to make difficult decisions they "weigh" the choices by thinking about things in favor of each choice. The choice with the more things in favor of it is the winner.

On the next page there is a Decision Scale. It looks like a seesaw, doesn't it? Cut out the Decision Blocks below and paste them on the side of the scale where you think they belong. Each block contains a statement. The side with the most blocks has the most points in favor of it. That side is the correct decision.

# DECISION BLOCKS

It will make the people I care about happy.

It is good for me.

It is the more important thing.

It is the responsible thing to do.

It will make me feel good about myself.

C-5

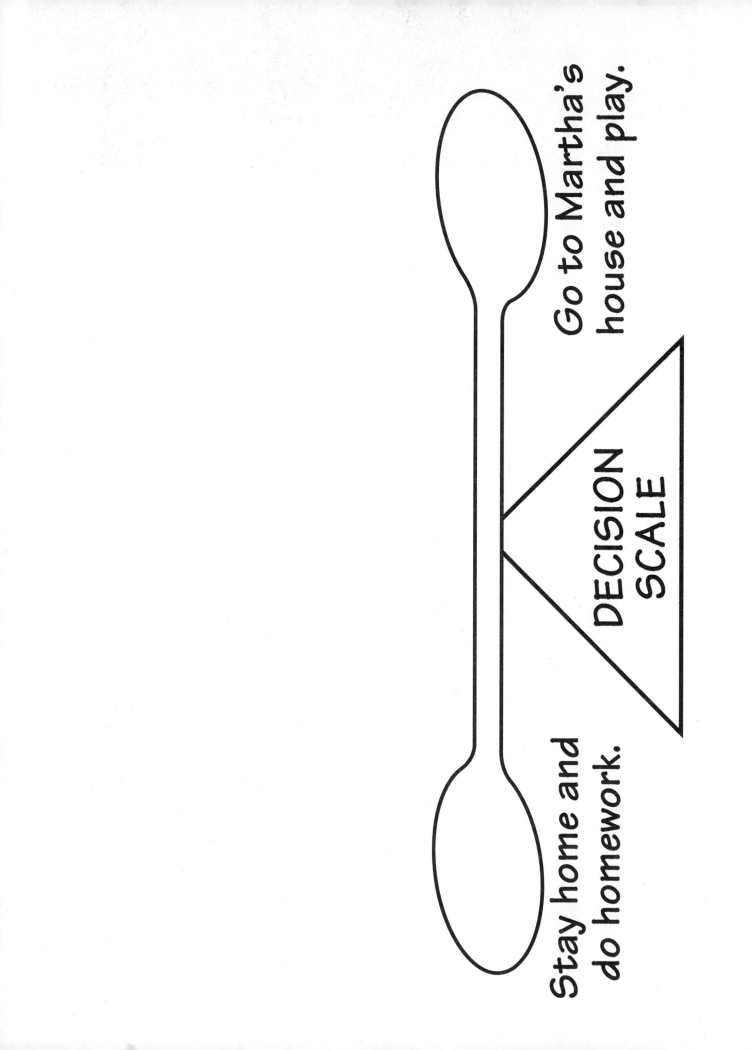

Henry was very jealous of Harry.

Harry got good grades, but Henry got only average grades because his work was always late or incomplete.

Harry was captain of the baseball team (and was the best player) because he practiced every afternoon. Henry only practiced once in a while, and sometimes he even showed up late for games.

Harry always had fun things to do on weekends, because he would start to think about what he wanted to do on Monday and he'd make plans with his friends to do them. Henry almost never had anything to do on weekends that was fun. He'd never even think about the weekend until he got up on Saturday morning, and by then everyone he knew was already busy. Most of the time he hung around his house by himself.

Henry was as smart, as nice, and as much fun as Harry. But there was one big difference: he never thought ahead and made any plans.
Can you help plan a week for Henry?

Paste in symbols for homework (pencil), baseball practice (baseball), chores (broom), and making plans with friends (phone) on the calendar on the next page. Write in anything else that you think Henry should plan to do.

C-6

| Sunday | Monday | Tuesday | Wednesday | Thursday | Friday | Saturday |
|--------|--------|---------|-----------|----------|--------|----------|
| morning | morning | morning | morning | morning | morning | morning |
| noon | noon | noon | noon | noon | noon | noon |
| night | night | night | night | night | night | night |

 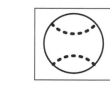 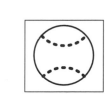   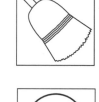

People who are successful usually have a positive attitude. They are aware of problems or difficulties, but they don't let negative thoughts keep them from trying to do their best.

Keeping negative thoughts away can be a battle for some people, and that is just what this game is about. You can help Gerald get rid of his negative thoughts.

**To Play:**

1. Make copies of the opposite page. You will need one copy for each time you play.

2. Get a pencil and hold it about one foot above the battleground on the next page.

3. You have 20 tries to "bomb" the negative tanks below by dropping the pencil on the tanks.

4. When your pencil hits the tank and makes a mark you can cross that tank off.

5. To win, you must hit all 10 tanks in 20 tries, protecting Gerald from negative thoughts. If you hit Gerald, you automatically lose.

(For non-readers: The adult should read the directions and the sayings on the tanks to the child and explain why negative thoughts are harmful).

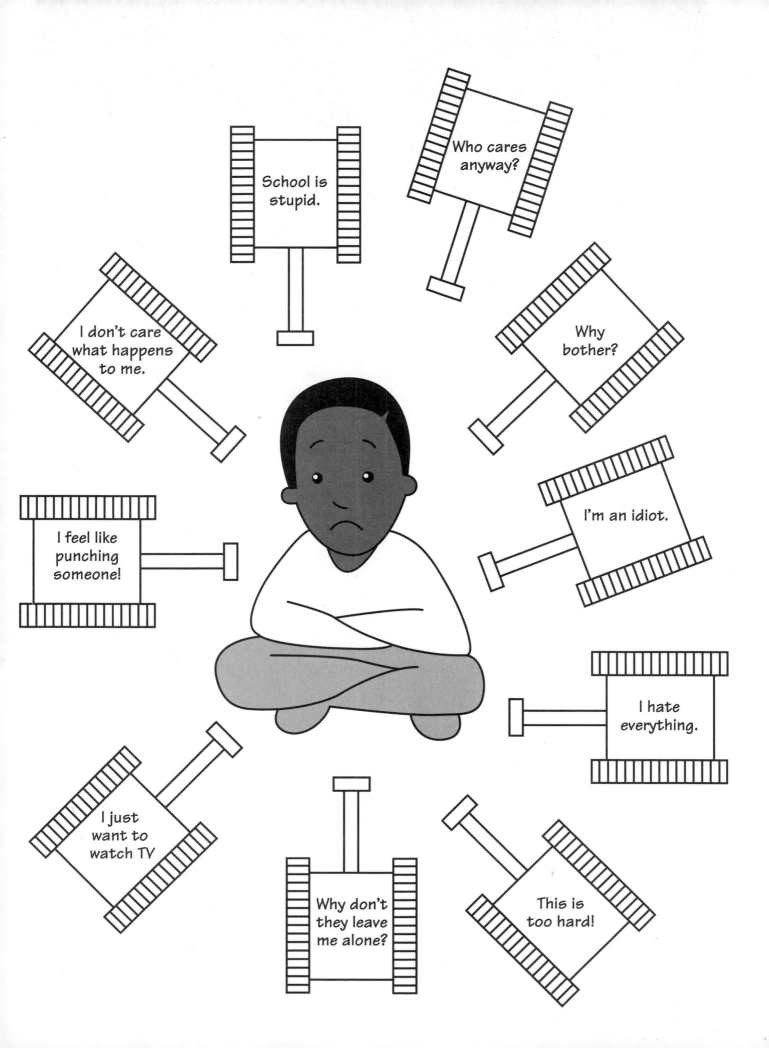

**Area: Cognition**
**Activity: The Power of Imagination**
**Objective: To see how imagination can be used to visualize success.**

Imagination is a great help in achieving your goals. Some people have said that picturing something in their mind (like running a movie in your mind) helps them to work toward a difficult goal:

*"I used to imagine myself graduating from college; getting my diploma in front of all my family and friends. I worked hard until I made that dream come true."*

or:

*"I used to practice the same basketball shot over and over again. I used to see it in my mind. And when it came time to make the shot, I did."*

But dreaming isn't enough. People need to work hard to achieve a goal. Draw yourself doing the things you need to do to achieve your goals below. Start at the lowest box and go toward the trophy.

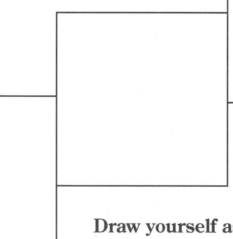

**Draw yourself as you imagine you would look, working to achieve a goal.**

C-8

Did you ever get up to bat while playing baseball and your coach said,

> "You can do it!"
> "Go get 'em!"
> "Knock one out of the ball park!"

Coaches encourage their players to try harder, and players even talk to themselves while they play to make themselves run faster or concentrate harder.

Talking to yourself can help you in other areas of your life, too. It can help you be less afraid of a shot from the doctor, it can help you concentrate on your studies even when you are tired, and it can help you feel better about yourself, even if other people are putting you down.

On the next two pages, Marvin has to take a difficult path on his way home from school. He must pass a mean dog, a bully, a kid offering him drugs, a busy street, and kids who want him to play by the railroad tracks. Paste in the things that Marvin should say to himself by each of these problem situations in the maze. Then follow the path to take Marvin home, saying these statements out loud when you pass them.

## COACHING STATEMENTS

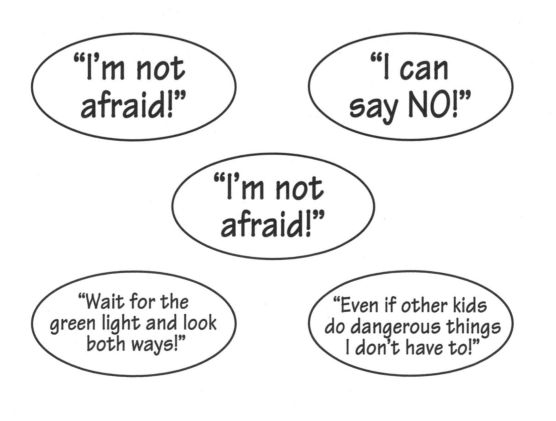

HOME

COGNITION

## Discussion Questions

1. Suppose you were taking a very long hike. You were getting tired, but you weren't nearly at the end yet. What could you say to yourself to give you the extra push to finish the hike?

2. Think of something that you really want to do, but you keep putting off. Is it a special project? A chore? Someplace you want to go? Now look at a calendar and pick a date to do whatever you have been putting off. Now make a list of the things that you need to do it.

3. Sometimes decisions are hard to make. But if you think them through, you can usually make the right choice. Ask a grown-up about a time he or she had to make a hard choice, but it turned out to be the right choice.

4. A dog will run after a rabbit. A donkey will follow carrot or an apple. What would make you do something that you had never done before?

5. "Think positively!" That's a phrase that always seems to help, even in the most difficult situation. Here are some negative words. Change them into positive ones and put them each in a sentence.

    *Can't. Won't. Afraid. Bad. Failure. Tired. Bored.*

6. Suppose you were going to plan a day-long hike. Why is it important to plan where you are going to go and what you are going to do? Can you name 10 things that you might want to take with you on a long hike in the mountains?

7. Sometimes when we feel badly about ourselves (*everyone* feels that way sometimes), it helps to remember a time when we felt very good. Can you get a "picture" of a really good time in your mind? Can you make the picture really clear? Tell exactly what you see.

8. There are many different kinds of decisions that we make. Some we can change easily, but others are very difficult to change once we have made them. For example, if you think it is going to be cold outside and you wear an extra sweater, you can always take it off later. But if you tell your best friend that you are not going to be her best friend anymore and that you want someone else for a best friend, then she might never forget that. Can you think of three decisions that you made which were easy to change and three that were very difficult to change?

9. Do you watch commercials on TV? Commercials often have a "slogan," a saying which makes it easy to remember the product. For example: "You've got the right one, baby, uh huh," "Just do it," and "It's the real thing." These slogans are very positive, because the makers of these products want you to remember them with good feelings. Can you make up a slogan about yourself—a catchy phrase, which describes your best qualities?

10. Do you know anyone who has a physical handicap? Someone who is blind, or deaf, or in a wheelchair? What would you say to someone with a handicap who was feeling frustrated because he or she felt different from other people?

Developmental psychology tells us that every aspect of a child's growth (physical, emotional, cognitive, social, language, and so on) unfolds in a predictable pattern related to a child's aging.  It is true that some children develop faster than others, and certainly some grow in atypical ways.  In general, however, children are expected to achieve certain developmental milestones at certain ages.

But how does this growth affect a child's self-image, and what happens if a child fails to achieve certain developmental tasks?  Some theorists suggest that if a developmental task is not resolved appropriately, it can have a life-long affect.  Others emphasize the uniqueness of each personality and the fluidity of development as children cope and compensate as they face different challenges at different stages.

But whether it is through natural maturation or through coping, as a child "masters" each developmental task, he increases his feelings of competency and self-worth, and when he notices that he has achieved below his peers, his sense of adequacy is threatened.

Has anyone ever said to you, *"Why don't you act your age?"*

That's annoying, isn't it? But they may have a point. Things that children did when they were younger may not be acceptable when they are older. Kids can get teased by other kids or yelled at by parents when they do things that are more typical of younger children. It may not be fair, but it is the way things are.

Can you name the things that these children still do that they shouldn't be doing anymore?

D-1

**Area: Developmental**
**Activity: Different Things For Different People**
**Objective: To understand how different "tools for living"**
**represent different age-related tasks.**

People use different things at different ages. For example, it would be silly if your mother went to work with a baby rattle. And most little children don't need a calculator.

The Henderson family went on a trip and packed everything in one big suitcase. When they got to the hotel all their things were jumbled up. Can you help them find their things? Draw a different color line from each of the items listed below to the family member you think it belongs to. (Hint: Some things could belong to more than one person).

Now circle the objects which could only belong to one member of the Henderson family. What do you use that could only belong to someone your age?

D-2

Think of someone you admire, and think of three ways you are like him or her.

Paste or draw a picture of yourself here.

Paste or draw a picture of the person you admire here.

Name three ways you are like the person you admire.

1. _____

2. _____

3. _____

D-3

As kids grow up they learn to do more and more things for themselves. They become more independent.

Some things kids learn to do aren't much fun, like picking up their clothes or doing hard chores. But there are many more things that kids really like as they become more independent, like sleeping at a friend's house, going shopping by themselves, earning extra money by mowing the lawn or shoveling the snow for neighbors.

Tom, however, couldn't see the point of becoming independent. He would say, *"My mother will do it anyway, so why should I bother?"*

Take a good look at Tom in his room. Can you find five things he didn't do? (The answers are upside down at the bottom of this page).

What are the things that you like to do that show you are independent?

_____

_____

_____

Answers: 1) tie his shoes 2) wash his face and hands 3) put his toys away 4) make his bed 5) practice his saxophone

D-4

Can you find four ways that these children have learned to be responsible? (The answers are upside down at the bottom of this page).

Answers: 1) *girl helping boy up from the floor* 2) *girl doing homework at desk* 3) *boy sweeping floor* 4) *girl holding dustpan*

"I'll never grow up!" That's what Peter Pan used to say. He wanted to be a boy forever, and never have to take on adult responsibilities and problems. But there are a lot of things that adults can do that kids can't, things that make being a grown-up just as great as being a kid.

Here is a picture of Paul and Patty Pringle's playroom. Can you find eight of their toys that represent things that grown-ups can do? (Answers are upside down at the bottom of this page.)

Answers: 1) bride and groom dolls - get married 2) baby doll - have children 3) toy car - drive 4) toy telephone - have their own telephone number 5) play money - earn a salary 6) toy house - own a home 7) football - be on a professional team 8) book - write a novel

This family looks unhappy because everyone has lost something in this room. Can you find what each person has lost? Who do you think lost what? Can you find all 10 things that are lost? (Keys, doll, truck, glove, purse, sock, boots, books, pet rabbit and toy mouse).

D-7

A mean kid at school said you're stupid.  Can you think of five people who think you're smart?  Paste or draw pictures of them below, and write their names under the pictures.

**Area: Developmental**
**Activity: What Older Kids Do**
**Objective: To understand how kids can solve problems differently as they get older.**

On the playground there is a big slide that you are afraid to go down. What could an older kid think about to make it easier for him to go down? Draw it in the box. Ask an older kid (or adult) if you can't think of anything.

D-9

## Discussion Questions

1. What is the earliest memory you have?

2. What do you think is the most important thing that older children know?

3. How old is "old?"

4. What do you think you will be like when you are 21 years old and you are legally "grown-up?"

5. Ask your parents to see pictures of them when they were children. Do you look like them? How do you think they were different as children?

6. Someday you'll probably be a parent, too. What do you think is the most important thing to know about being a parent? If you don't know, ask!

7. Think about the other children in your class. Is there something that you can you do better than anyone else? (Maybe you aren't the fastest runner or the best at reading, but maybe you're the best artist, or the nicest person, or you can make the funniest face...).

8. If you had a time machine and you could go back to any age that you were or any age that you are going to be, where would you go, and what do you think you would see?

9. Martha loved her blanket when she was a baby. She loved it so much that she hated to be away from it. When she was old enough to go to school, she cut a little piece of it and she took it in her backpack with her to school. When she grew up and got a job, she still carried a piece of her blanket in her purse. Do you think that this was okay?

10. When you grow older, your interests change. Things that you liked to play with when you were younger may no longer interest you. Can you think of three things that you used to play with, but no longer play with, and three things that you like now, but you will probably not like in five years?

Children are egocentric when they are born, and this continues through the first years of their lives. Growing up is a process of learning to temper one's self-interest with the interest of others; balancing gratification with altruism. But how do children learn to keep this balance?

They must be taught.

Values must be taught at every stage of a child's life, both formally and informally. Social values are, of course, paramount. When a child extends himself to others, acts considerately, or behaves responsibly, he has an immediate sense of "doing the right thing," which contributes immeasurably to his sense of self.

Aesthetic values are also important. Music, literature, the arts, the beauty of nature, are all important to a higher sense of one's "being," and give a meaning to life which can transcend the day-to-day difficulties that often wear us down.

If you were stranded on a deserted island but you had the three things that were most important to you, what would they be? Draw them in below (or paste them from a magazine).

E-1

If you had three wishes, *but they had to be used to help someone else*, what would they be?

I wish for:

1. _____
2. _____
3. _____

E-2

What are some of the things that you or your family members have done that you are most proud of?  Fill in the newspaper headlines below so that they describe these terrific events.

**Example:**

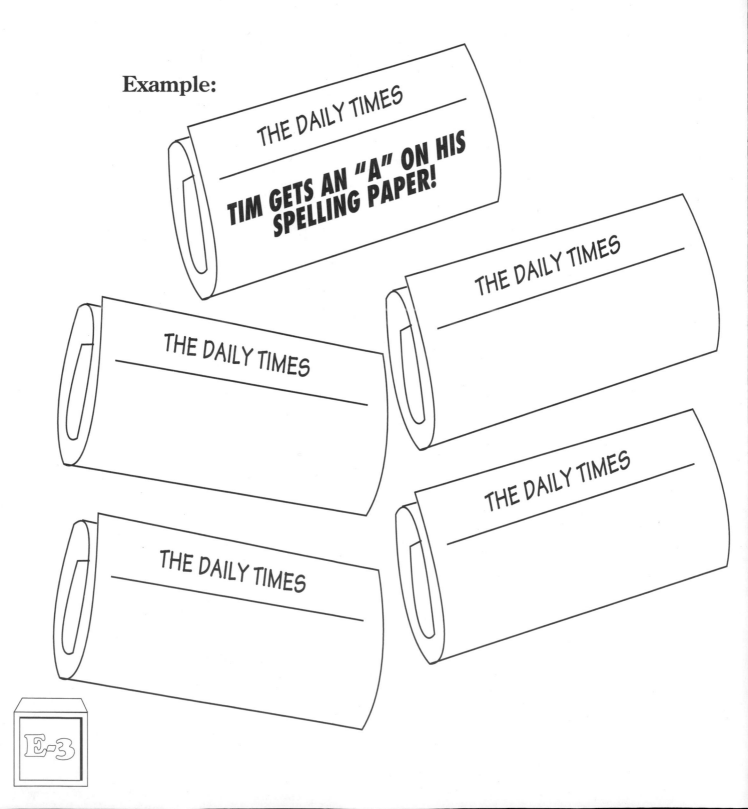

THE DAILY TIMES

TIM GETS AN "A" ON HIS SPELLING PAPER!

THE DAILY TIMES

THE DAILY TIMES

THE DAILY TIMES

THE DAILY TIMES

There are many problems in the world that affect a lot of children. Many children don't have enough food. Others may not be able to go to school. Pollution is bad in some places and will get worse as today's children become adults.

The President of the United States is elected by the people of our country, and he wants to know what you think our most important problems are. Why don't you write him a letter and send it to the White House? Who knows, he may even answer your letter!

## Dear Mr. President,

These are some of the things that I am worried about and would like you to work on.

1. _____

2. _____

3. _____

4. _____

5. _____

Signed _____

E-4

Family meetings can be an important time to talk about problems that you are having. Most of the time other family members can help you with your problems.

Tara is having a problem learning to read. Everyone seems to be a better reader than she is. What do you think the family is saying to her? Write it in or have someone write it in for you.

A lot of people don't like the way they look. They think that they are too short, or too fat, or have a funny looking nose...or something else.

But nobody's perfect, and most of the time we have to learn to like ourselves just the way we are.

One of the problems has to do with what we think we are "supposed" to look like. We see a lot of people on TV and in the movies and in magazines who are "almost" perfect. But they are professional models and actors, and even they don't look that perfect in real life.

Get some magazines and cut out pictures of models who you think are really beautiful. Then get some magazines and cut out pictures of some *real* people. Paste them on the next two pages.

Then take a marker and circle the features or body parts that you think you really will have when you grow up—not the way you want to look, but the way you really will look! (Take a look at your relatives. Who do you look like now? You may look even more like them when you grow up.)

Paste pictures of models here.

Paste pictures of the way people *really* look here.

Television can have a very powerful influence on the way we think and act.

Some people think that children who see a lot of violence on TV will be more violent themselves.

Some people think that kids shouldn't watch certain shows because they will upset them or show them things that they won't understand.

Below and on the next page are six television sets.  In the first three, draw or write in the names of TV shows that you think are *good* for kids to watch.

In the second three televisions, draw or write in the names of TV shows that you think kids *shouldn't* watch.

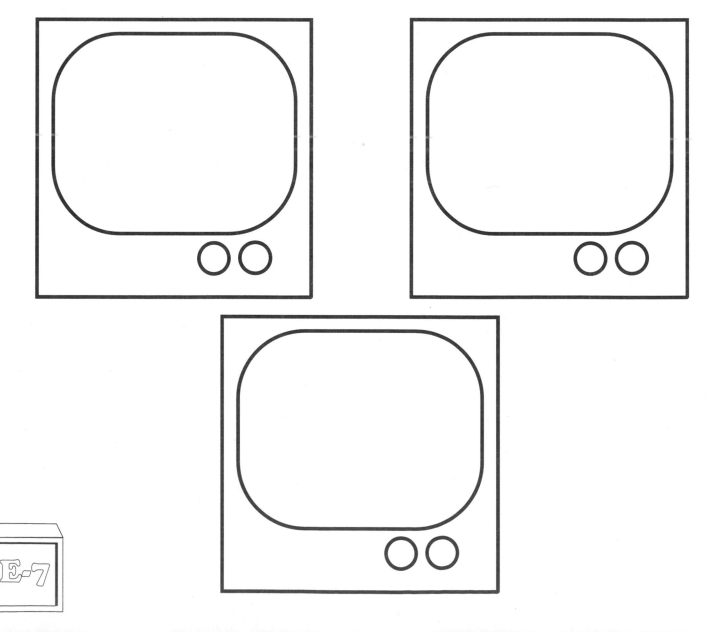

FAMILY TV GUIDE

Kids love to watch TV, but too much TV isn't good for you. Who makes the rules about TV watching in your family? What are they? Write them down in your FAMILY TV GUIDE.

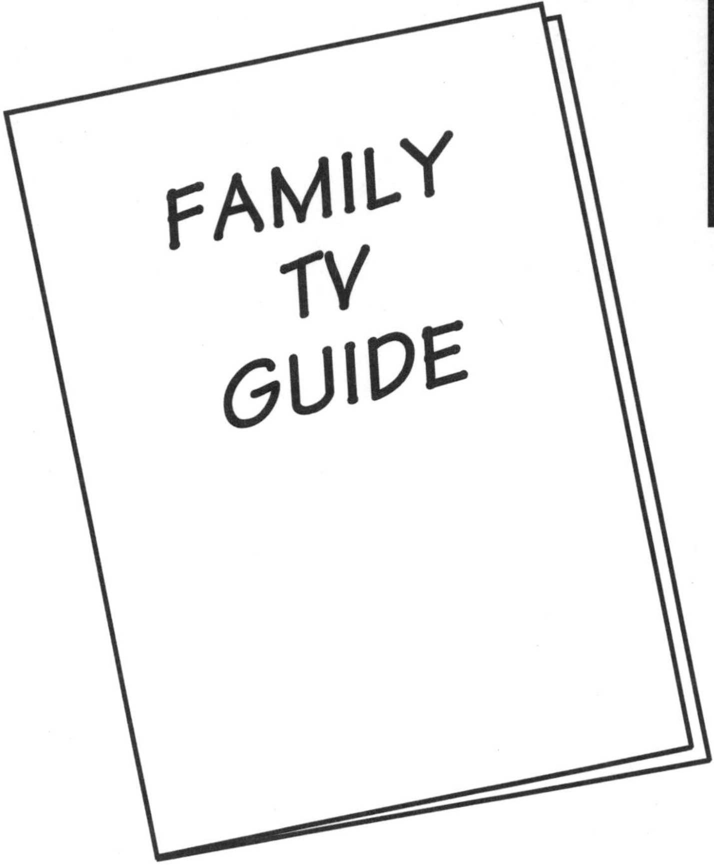

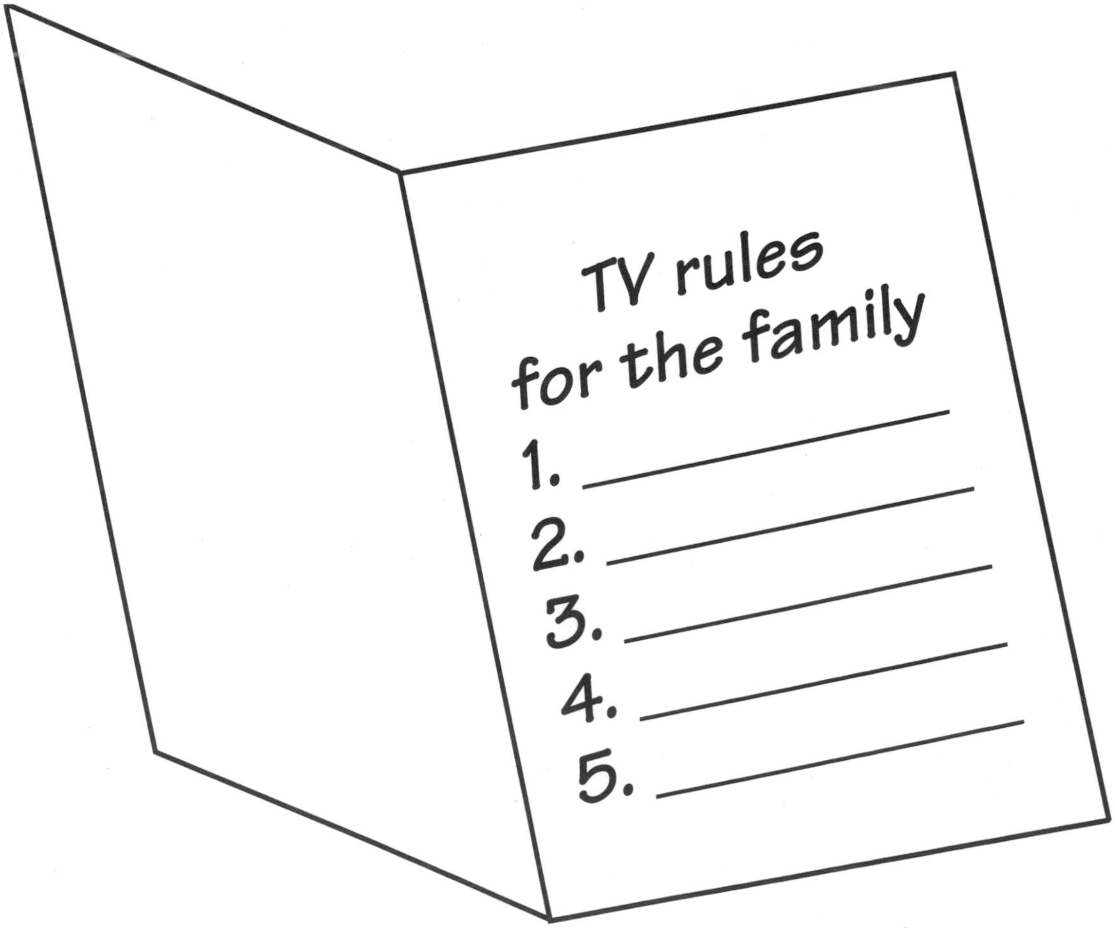

TV rules
for the family

1. _____

2. _____

3. _____

4. _____

5. _____

E-8

Write in something your mom has told you that made you feel like you were a *responsible* person.

## Area: Education
## Activity: A Family Garden of Values
## Objective: To identify positive family values.

Families are a lot like gardens. They need to be tended, fed, and nurtured to produce strong and healthy people. Below is your "family garden." Have each family member plant something that they think the family needs to grow. We've started the picture for you by planting some love.

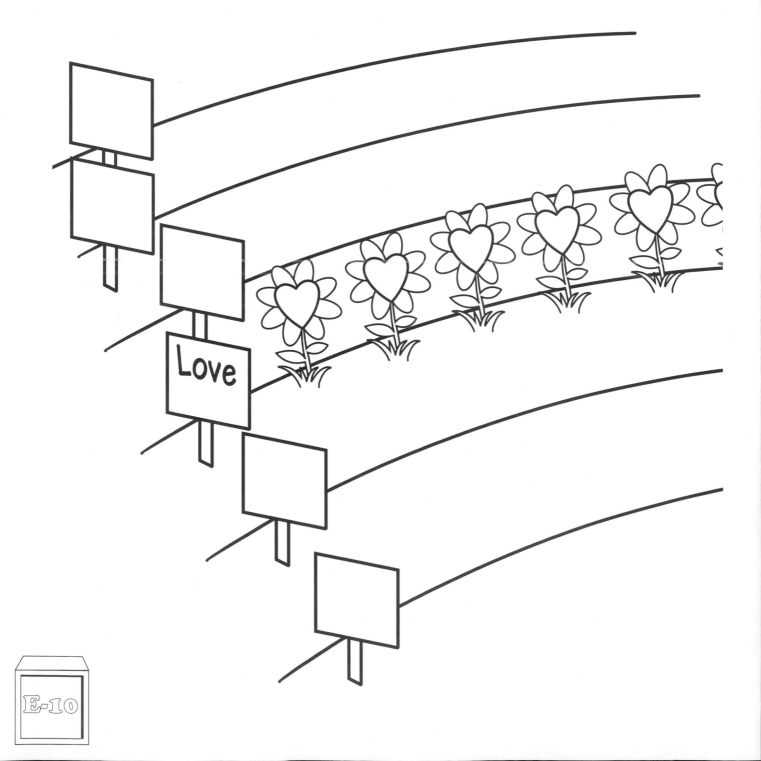

Love

E-10

## Discussion Questions

1. What is the nicest thing that you ever did for someone else?

2. What do you think should happen to companies that pollute?

3. Mary was walking to school one day when she saw a bird with a broken wing on the sidewalk. She wanted to help, but she was late for school, and her mother had told her, "Never touch a strange animal." What do you think she did?

4. If you won a million dollars in the lottery, what would you do with it?

5. Why do you think people go to art museums?

6. Some people say that "nature" is more beautiful than anything that people could ever create. What do you think is the most beautiful thing in nature?

7. If you saw a homeless person on the street asking for money for food, what would you do?

8. If you knew a child who felt bad about himself because he was "different," what would you do?

9. Charity—giving something that belongs to you to someone else who needs it—is very important. Can you find something that belongs to you that might be helpful to someone else and give it to him?

10. Why is it important to respect older people?

It would be difficult to overemphasize the importance of a child's social system in developing self-esteem. The family, of course, is the primary influence. But as a child becomes school-aged, his or her peers can exert a profound influence as well. For some children, people in the community—coaches, religious leaders, even neighbors—can also have an important influence.

Other people influence a child's self-esteem in many ways. They can have a negative influence, in terms of rejection, prejudice, even abuse, but they can also provide nurturance, encouragement, acceptance, friendship, roles to model, and many more positive qualities.

# Area: Social Skills
## Activity: Getting Help
## Objective: To identify "helping" people in the community.

There are many people who can help you with things like schoolwork, or getting to important places, or when you are in trouble. Draw a line from each person to the problem they can help you with.

S-1

When Tommy was new in school he was not sure how to make friends.  As he thought about it, he drew some pictures of things to remind himself later.  But when "later" came, Tommy's dog had eaten half the page.  Can you tell what pictures Tommy drew?  What was he going to do with each thing he drew to help him make new friends?

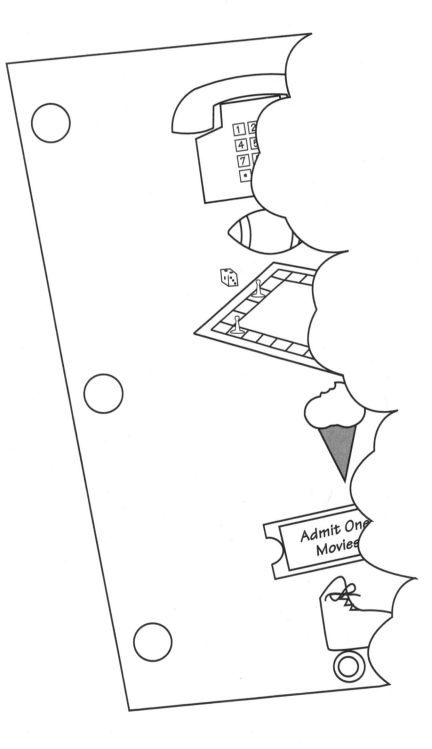

S-2

One way people express their feelings is by sending cards. Cards can say a lot about how we feel about our friends and family. Look at the cards below and on the next page and fill in a message on the inside of each card.

There is a new kid in your classroom. Can you think of some things that you can say to make her feel welcome? Write them in the "speech balloons."

Betty is one of the happiest and best-liked kids we know. What is it about Betty that makes her so popular? Let's follow her through one day and see what she does. Below each picture, write down what Betty is doing to make other people like her.

_____

_____

4+4=8
7+3=10

S-5

_____   _____   _____

You've probably heard the expression, "Be a good sport."  It means that no matter whether you win or lose at a game, it is important to be considerate and thoughtful of the other person with whom you are playing.  It is more important to have fun than to win.

Here is a funny game you can play with a friend.  Each of you should start at the beginning of one of the mazes.  *But the object of this game is to let the other person finish the maze first!*  Who will be the most polite?  Who will be the most thoughtful?

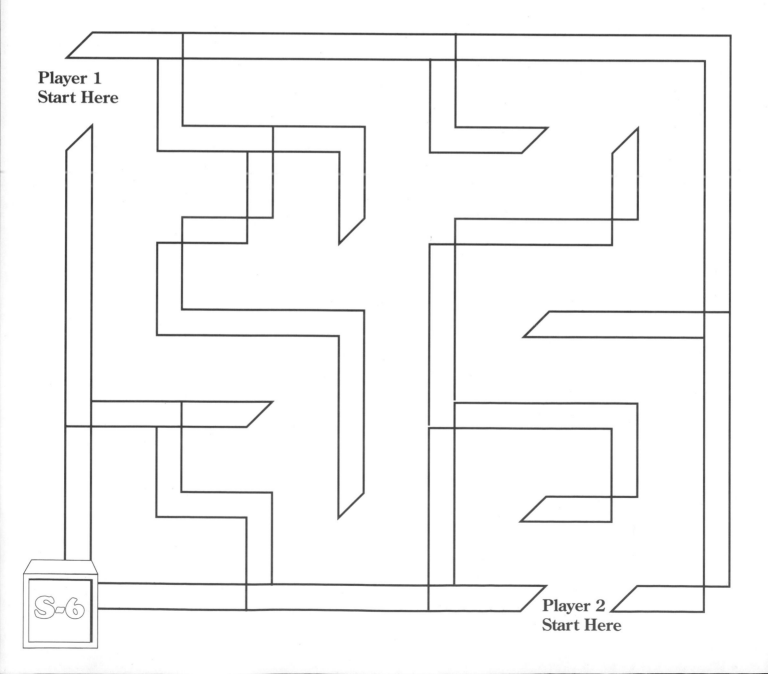

**Player 1**
**Start Here**

**Player 2**
**Start Here**

S-6

**Player 1
Start Here**

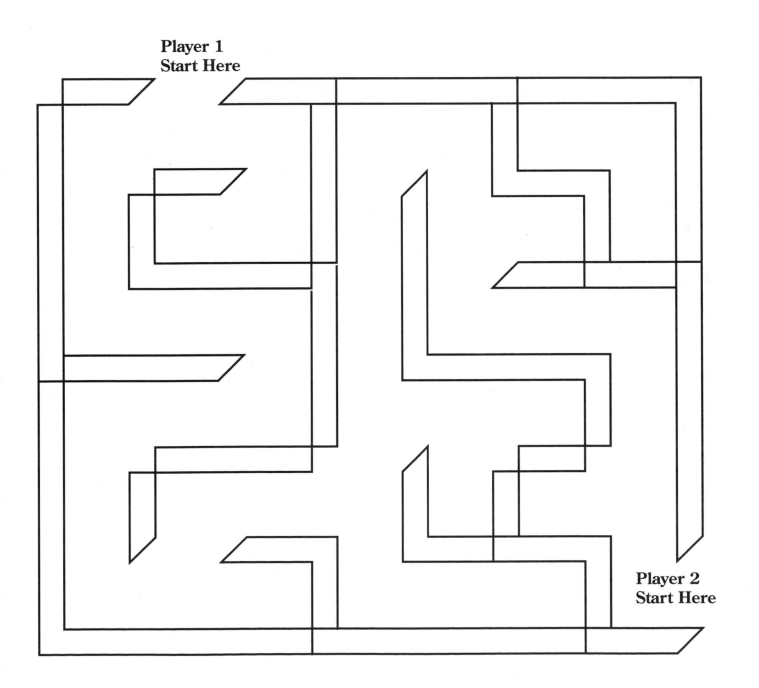

**Player 2
Start Here**

Here are five sets of identical twins. They are exactly alike, but one of each of the twins has the traits of a leader and the other is more of a follower. Can you tell by looking at each of the twins which one is the leader? (Answers are upside down at the bottom of this page).

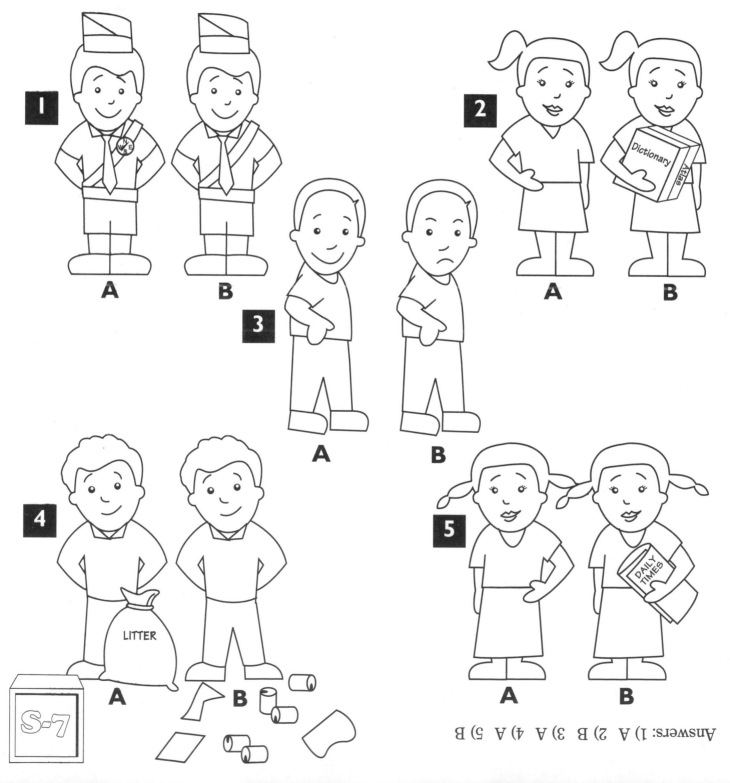

S-7

Mary and her friends wanted to start a club. Mary was a very organized person, and she made a list of six things that needed to be done. But when she was telling her best friend Sheila about the list, she realized she had left it at home. Mary could remember what was on the list, but she couldn't remember the correct order of the things that had to be done!

Can you help her by putting her ideas in the correct order? Put the correct number (1 - 7) by each picture showing the correct order of the steps to start a club.

S-8

An important part of who you are comes from the groups that you belong to. Maybe you are a boy scout, or you belong to a church group. Your class is a group and so is your family. Maybe you are African American or Italian American. Do you belong to the group of people who wear glasses? Or the group of people who are baseball fans?

Write all the groups you belong to below.

1. _____

2. _____

3. _____

4. _____

5. _____

6. _____

7. _____

8. _____

9. _____

10. _____

11. _____

12. _____

Now draw in a picture of yourself with something that represents each of these groups in the boxes on the next page. (For example: a baseball cap, clothes that are typical of your background, etc.)

Do you know the story of Dr. Frankenstein?  He created a person from various parts of other people lying around his laboratory.  Unfortunately, his creation was seen as a *monster* and was not particularly good company.

Suppose you could create a best friend for yourself.  What would he or she be like?  Mix and match parts of people on the next page to create your own best friend or use pictures from a magazine.  Cut out the parts you like and paste them in the frame on this page.  Do you know someone almost like the person you created?

After you draw in the face and clothes, draw in anything else that you think might give your friend "personality," such as a football, a phone, a pencil, glasses, etc.

"My Best Friend"

**Area: Social Skills**
**Activity: Getting the Point of View**
**Objective: To understand that people can have different points of view depending on their immediate and past experiences.**

The way you think and feel about things often depends on your point of view. If you just had a huge piece of cake you would probably feel differently about eating a bowl of ice cream than someone who had spent the day outside and hadn't eaten a thing all day.

These photographs were taken by six different people. Can you match the photograph with each person by drawing a line from the correct person to the photo?

S-11

## Discussion Questions

1. Who is your best friend? Why?

2. If you had your own club, what would you call it, and who would you invite to be in it?

3. Why do you think that some kids become bullies?

4. Who in your family makes the rules?

5. Name three people in your community who can help you if you are in trouble.

6. Name some "leaders" you know. What does it mean to be a leader?

7. How do you know when someone is a good friend?

8. When someone makes you angry, what can you do about it?

9. Betty went to Mava's birthday party, but when she got there she realized that she had forgotten to bring a gift. What could she do or say to make Mava understand?

10. If one of your friends seemed sad and upset all the time, but didn't want to talk about it, what would you do?

# MORE SELF-ESTEEM BUILDERS FROM

### ALL FEELINGS ARE OK—IT'S WHAT YOU DO WITH THEM THAT COUNTS

- Teaches children that learning to recognize and talk about one's feelings is important
- Unique workbook gives kids the chance to express their feelings as they are asked how they feel about everyday occurrences
- One face in every illustration is blank so that they can either stamp or draw in the face that best expresses their feelings
- Comes with four Feelings Faces stamps, non-toxic ink pad, crayons and sheet of 34 Feelings Faces

**#7432  $23.95**

### TAKE A DEEP BREATH:
**The Kids' Play-Away Stress Book**

- Teaches children aged 4 through 10 what stress is and how to deal with it
- Includes activities, non-toxic clay and boy and girl cookie cutters for creative play
- Written by child psychologists

**#7000  $19.95**

### ALL ABOUT DIVORCE

- Gives children honest answers to their important questions about how their families may change
- Comes with a doll family and back-drop scenes to allow children to play out their concerns
- Includes written activities to help children express and share their feelings

**#7002  $19.95**

### SOMETIMES I DRIVE MY MOM CRAZY, BUT I KNOW SHE'S CRAZY ABOUT ME

- A warm, humorous and highly-accurate portrayal of an ADHD child
- Specifically addresses self-esteem problems of ADHD children
- Details tried-and-true interventions such as behavioral programs, educational management, parent support groups, role models, medication and more
- Includes behavior charts for helping ADHD children
- Includes a comprehensive list of resources for helping ADHD children
- Written by a child psychologist

**#7400  $14.95**